One Wild Word Away

One Wild Word Away

Poems

by Geffrey Davis

AMERICAN POETS CONTINUUM SERIES NO. 207

BOA EDITIONS, LTD. * ROCHESTER, NY * 2024

First Edition
23 24 25 26 7 6 5 4 3 2 1

For information about permission to reuse any material from this book, please contact The Permissions Company at www.permissionscompany.com or e-mail permdude@gmail.com.

Publications by BOA Editions, Ltd.—a not-for-profit corporation under section 501 (c) (3) of the United States Internal Revenue Code—are made possible with funds from a variety of sources, including public funds from the Literature Program of the National Endowment for the Arts; the New York State Council on the Arts, a state agency; and the County of Monroe, NY. Private funding sources include the Max and Marian Farash Charitable Foundation; the Mary S. Mulligan Charitable Trust; the Rochester Area Community Foundation; the Ames-Amzalak Memorial Trust in memory of Henry Ames, Semon Amzalak, and Dan Amzalak; the LGBT Fund of Greater Rochester; and contributions from many individuals nationwide. See Colophon on page 75 for special individual acknowledgments.

Cover Art: "Boy Owl" by Kevin Foote
Cover Design: Sandy Knight
Interior Design and Composition: Isabella Madeira
BOA Logo: Mirko

BOA Editions books are available electronically through BookShare, an online distributor offering Large-Print, Braille, Multimedia Audio Book, and Dyslexic formats, as well as through e-readers that feature text to speech capabilities.

Cataloging-in-Publication Data is available from the Library of Congress.

BOA Editions, Ltd.
250 North Goodman Street, Suite 306
Rochester, NY 14607
www.boaeditions.org
A. Poulin, Jr., Founder (1938-1996)

Contents

for Carlos

Time Can't Erase, Together

Unlike a grave, I plant love well inside
the green field of this poem, a breathing
to be carried back or stay safely buried
until the next nodding light.   Or, unlike

a grave, the body of this poem will not
remain buried in our understanding
of loss, an unfinished bridge now love can
stunt across to deliver the new myths

from its shaking arms.   —Just like a grave,
some distances become a mouth's darkness
when opened by the verge of pain that could
be pleasure.   —Just like a grave, reach without touch

might unstitch the old wounds.   But what absence
cannot bury is the body of love.

From the Midnight Notebooks

—for L

Dearly Beloved—Remission means
you need real rest, but fear

unleashes another quiet

or not-so-quiet litany of reasons
to spit the bullet of sleep.

Cancer keeps your mind

backfiring deep into the night:
& if I perish?   & what of hope?

& of family?   & of desire?

With time on my breath,
I offer the first lullaby I believe

could sing you beyond any cold

idea inside our bed: *I love all the ways
you haven't died yet…*

**

Dearly Beloved—Of course sleep finds you,
& how terrible now my wish for your ear

as the causeway that would clear

the darkly stalled traffic of—yes—my heart.
From the sound of it, already your breathing lies

among the soft yonder.   & while I try

to stay in love with the slumber I guess
has tucked you inside the safe

half-afterlife of unconsciousness, I also want

the tender otherness of your hearing to reveal
a question less dangerous than the night's.

Forgive this lonely draw against our union-whole.

Call it *failure* or *trauma* or—how long until you wake
& banish the new brutality of my uncertainty?

**

Dearly Beloved—I am remembering
the day we kissed time

into its unbroken helix

of chance, confirming how to be made
mostly of water means we mirror

the many distances of rain & not

the fragile singularity of any
stunning reflection distilled

by a passing storm.

But who can resist all doubt
with lightning's one myth overhead?

My voice would break through the night

to rewrite each flash reflected
in the peril of your upturned eyes.

**

Dearly Beloved—I have gathered
before our darkened window

to decipher tomorrow

when more thunder begins
to trouble the distant air.

As wind continues

blurring the space
between threat & arrival,

I feel how far apart

our living was destined
to seem someday—& for

long enough to risk naming it

something grace should survive,
I didn't look away…

**

Dearly Beloved—What too
shall pass, & why tonight—

this movement like water

calling the barely desired dark?
When will our bed sound

less of weeping: vivid

then weak
then blue all over?

Who made the memory

of a funeral with few flowers
cross the decades?

How do I accept

a future for light
with this life not yet saved?

**

Dearly Beloved—There's nothing I've learned
to fear more than the sound love can make

when punching its exit from a life.

—Once upon a time, you were dying.
—Once, a surgeon returned your unfinished name.

—Then, for survival, a surgeon knifed our vision

of future children. Since then, I've heard you
burying your body-song below that last surrender,

& so the low hum of recovery keeps bewildering,

keeps hitting too near the parting possibility.
Can I follow & find your blood-engine still

knocking toward the hardship of belief?

Can we reclaim the night without another
hymn to convince us of our staying?

**

Dearly Beloved—No such body here.
No such body. No such body here. No

such body. No such body here. No such

body. No such body here. No such body.
No such body here. No such body. No

such body here. No such body. No such

body here. No such body. No such body
here. No such body. No such body here.

No such body.

No such body here. No such body here.
No such body. No such body.

But here, Beloved.

& Dearly.   Such Beloved & such here.
Such Dearly here.

**

Dearly Beloved—We've had enough
evenings without the word *oblivion*

sharpening the living-room air

to rekindle some warm faith
in *together.*   Let us try

any ritual designed

to unsing an early elegy.
No chord could cleave

your light from our story!

No throat could close around
the cold imaginary of your absence!

—Not without converting…

—Not without answering the sudden
godliness of your dark forever…

Separated

no ode to rupture
beyond the dark irreverence
for facing down how hope fails
I will admit
all the sorry facts
my beloved & I survived
bitternesses that did not sever
the days we had
of figuring a way
with our histories of grief
—then the fetal pulse faltered…
which could've but
for death's unknowable bottom
shattering our original longing
what with weeping I can call a miracle
quietly flooding the shared rooms
goddamn *time*   pulling us
I don't want
bewilderment left in the wake
after a torn wander

I prayed for a new grace
in my hands & voice
first—though
I tended to claim
the losses
both rare & usual
how we fevered
the early months
to fit *love* in the mouth
still feral behind our teeth
—then her cancer…
didn't take her
so I tried blessing every ragged thing
reshaping our tomorrow
each revised gravity of light
I know   I know
into the actual ending
to become an ugly
waiting
until some last silence

&

I don't want her alone either inside
the absurdity that we
wove into *home*   our reckless desire
divided—what future shudder
my god   I need it to matter then
of so many evenings   swaying to
a hurt-close living   smiling & turning

whatever field follows
being wild with *faith*
to rise together & not feel
did we dream for one another
how we outlasted the darkness
the temporary music made by
the entire night sometimes   fixed

according to the brief
but unbroken tracks of joy
the doom of our loaded hearts could sing

Aubade

Beyond my door, no end to cricketing. What else but ceaselessness could answer
the different doubts divided by the dark? How long would you dare

your throat

to hold against a body's whirring uncertainty without cure?
When pure light stalls the singing, my mind begins to build

a shadow

chorus from that muted music of desire.
And if it starts again, I want my ear

to drop

all invention to be back inside
that cinched galaxy…

that singular sigh…

Sonnet With Its Breath Knocked Out

Mess

Mass

Miss

Muss

Moss
Moss

21

How to Stay Sorry

Sometimes you are the storm.

        Sometimes you are just *in* the storm,
              wind darkening your vision.

      Sometimes you are just *before* the storm, flash-claps
             louder than each prayer you have
             for staring down its image.

            Until it howls back, sometimes you stay
in love with the storm, and swear to seeing the face
of your future still written
across the clouds of its departure.

Sometimes the storm marches you hundreds of miles, each step
throbbing with *change*, only to recognize the old dangers
gathering in the private brilliance of a bathroom mirror.

Sometimes, instead of home, you call the storm, guided by questions you believe
might protect you from your wounded life—how do our hands make a safety?

Sometimes the storm finds its way inside, turns your chest into a hidden hive that
even the smoke from a lightning strike would not clear from your heart.

             Sometimes you are the storm.

Nuclear

—after Kamilah Aisha Moon

Like love, anger
can make a star
        of your presence—
    voice spun down
by pain's own
        undeniable pull,
    even tenderness
altered into the imminent
        heat of scrutiny;

    & if tinier than
our sun—no core
        to collapse around,
    no mass to glow beyond
an ignorable red—
        that burn could last
    the quiet years:

a brilliant nebula
        of gravity
    failing to die.

Regard the glare.

Longing, We Say

—for S

Because isn't it enough to just hold one voice,
I placed the raw wonder of my ear
beneath a friend's ruined marriage, its sudden long lack.

>   (Tears that left her loveliness
>   fed the yard rioting at her feet.)

So when a lone robin perched near
and, with last light, set its own ragged notes of grief
to cutting the warm air around us, I
had nothing but hope for that bird.

>   (My eyes returned to my friend's eyes,
>   my hand to the hard wind at her back.)

If the world is a sacred song, fractured
by desire's difficult half-names, loneliness
heightened with each lucid yearning...   Let us hold just one voice.

Loom

"Everyone forgets that Icarus also flew." —Jack Gilbert

Before this bedroom window,
        the idea of wings begins to thin.

Before this bedroom window,
        I hear what I know
        tried to ground me—
        what could've but didn't
        drown out the old myths.

Before this bedroom window,
        another blue maw
        opens for my suffering, trust
        rumbling the belly of this house.

Before this bedroom window,
        so much sounds
        like the trouble with flight.

**

Before this new window,
        the rescued dog feels unseen.

Before this new window,
        the rescued dog tears down
        a woodpile that took days
        to gather for future fires.

Before this new window,
        the dog starts another undoing
        between the one I'd imagined.

Before this new window,
        without perfect words for peace,
        the dog dozes, half-framed by
        branches & a sunlight throwing
        its weightless brunt just the same.

**

Before this opened window,
            the warm wind.

Before this opened window,
            the warm wind &
            the grandstanding leaves.

Before this opened window,
            the warm wind &
            the grandstanding leaves
            collaborate to sound like a memory.

Before this opened window,
            the warm wind &
            the grandstanding leaves
            & the memory of a rain
            that didn't fall.

**

Before this window flooded with light,
                a discord of jubilation.

Before this window flooded with light,
                the switchgrass & the wildflowers,
                the summer-drunk wasp-song,
                the summer-drunk bird-song.

Before this window flooded with light,
                a symphony made vast
                by possibility.

Before this window flooded with light,
                the backyard brandishes
                its many voices, a honeyed dispute
                I will dare my ear's tender fabric
                to recognize as *home*.

**

Before this,

      the cicadas continue to cry.

Before this,

      the many accidents of liftoff.

Before this,

      no amens louder than tomorrow.

Before this,

      a fierce horizon of never knowing.

Before this,

      yesterday's small addition to eternity.

Before this,

      children laughing in the near distance.

Before this,

      enough harmony to call it singing.

Self-Portrait With Waiting

The first time I saw fog
      rewrite a river's face,
            matter's transformation

      offered its myth about
            change—so I converted
to The Church of Family

Salvation. I stashed away
            my dearest hallelujahs
for my addict-father's

            return from the sick clouds,
      his stormy hands anchored
in safety and loyal now

      to staunching
an Old Testament absence.
            I even tried praying

            against all other longings
      until I felt nothing
      but scorned hope.

As it turns out, no grace
can give you permission
to redeem the better light

      of someone else's name.
      But who hasn't been hurt
            by The Good Book of Faith,

            or by mirrors silvered
before our shattered belief
      in becoming?

It Must Have Been Summer

—after Dorianne Laux

In our childhood there were cousins:
blood cousins and cousins inducted
by the bonds of aunties, by the proximity
of poverty and play,
even a girl who seemed to arrive on our doorstep
to bury her own last name...
—And one boy who was older
and babysat us, slipped my younger siblings
candy before meals but chose only to add
a new scythe to my posture. My father
was a defensive feen who had tried
once or twice to pin my life to his
genesis of drugs, so I knew enough
to rent my body to pain. Just another
addict's child who'd learned to stop
asking for mercy. We must have made
a startling two-headed thing: the older boy's
black curls unfurling from his baseball cap
as he dragged the spade of his tongue
against my naked back, though no one
would have seen us, not a window
looking down into the basement
he led me to in the middle of the afternoon.
It must have been summer,
I was seven or eight, no fathom or fuse
in my heart for ascending
the stairs, for running the impossible miles back
home across the city or crawling to where
my mother labored to wash
hunger's reek from her children's minds.
He must have been fifteen or sixteen, I can recall
the cold flare of the concrete at my chest,

even through the pallet of blankets
he lay beneath me, and then the animal
of his lust upon that, the gravel
of puberty and worry knocking around
inside his voice, tender with me under
the living-room floor, unlike in the blame of light
where he'd pebble me with shame to cover
the darkness he was making of desire.
It was 1990 or '91, he claimed me
as his favorite with the same breath
fueling the sinew that slid
my underwear the skinny length
of my hairless legs. I'd never heard
a sound more lost than my father
except my mother. Radio stations spun
Boyz II Men and Mariah Carey's
"Vision of Love," the movie theaters
were showing *Beauty and the Beast*,
there was trouble in Kuwait, space probes
sending back smaller and smaller perspectives
on Earth's blue dazzle. Eventually
I'd have hands as strong as his, El Niño
setting power-seizing storms
into motion along the coast. He finished
what was started and, without more words,
climbed back into the ignorance of the day
while I waited in a tilted dark
until the depth of someone else's worry
began to raise my old name.

The Simile Problem

I.

the hurt	I thought
was done	by me
before	knowing
the word	abuse

beats like

a bright	jay's wings
against	the cold
veil but	which side
opens	to release

II.

I do	just as
like it	the light
sometimes	nearly
better	goes out

on me

wearing	I think
a new	most doubt
music	back down
again	to quiet

The Metaphor Problem

Admittedly a little in love with the glint
inside their laughter, I tell the table of young writers

how, during my brief stint as a 4-H farm boy,
the black lamb I'd been given had this habit

of dragging my small body through the wood-bark
of a showroom arena. I make myself

into a cartoon of pain and holding on
to get my point across—*for weeks* I forgot

to simply let the damn sheep go; *for weeks*
I coughed on giant clouds of dust as its barnyard

breakout hoofed gobs of pine-scented chips
toward my sorry head, attached to my sorry arms

of never letting go. We shut our eyes
to step through the thought bubble of days gone.

I say I smell sweet feed and hay again,
which helps to shrink me further back

to an eight-year-old thinness, my weight
nothing close to what I needed

for wrangling a fearful mammal's instincts
to buck from becoming the circus act.

This ruminant rumpus, even after
my many hours of primping its fine wool

into county fair royalty. This beastly betrayal,
even after I'd risked bleating

an embarrassed handful of syllables
into the fleecy cup of its ear: *We*

and *Same* and *Safe*. From this quirky vantage
on history, I invite the writers

and I to chuckle at the absurdity of all
we've tried to tame with naming.

Then, remembering the lesson
about metaphor's ability to swerve

for new passengers, I confess
I'm bumping into humor's darker kin now—

how scary it feels to start seeing
that I will clench almost any image

if only to carry the difficult beauty
of a loved one's fallen face, long enough

to be picking splinters from my heart's knees
for weeks, that sting a familiarity to hold

closer until, no matter my desire, those thorns
work their way from beneath the skin

of my awareness. The writers have stopped
laughing with me. They do or do not reach

to soothe whatever jagged joke has just
brushed them on the shoulder. I want to trust,

despite the ring of worry in the room,
we have become both buckled

and reckless and at least one dark turn
readier to drive a future stretch

along the sharp roads of our reckoning.

Mercy from the Orchard

—for my brothers

To know a sweetness beyond reason,
before banishment, I scythed at the memories:
our father's clouded mind, his tendency
for tearing holes through home once the cravings
had turned his loveliness to smoke. But pity
can compromise a hard pruning. And hope
will leave its own hollow. The moment
I had nothing but violence for that man,
I dreamt an unbroken season of warmth
to cull each cold sorriness he had buried
inside our family's plot. And so, for years,
I remained guilty of denying winter's
proper rest. Then another field of grief

swept our mother's face—more children seeing
the hands of parents folded into fist-shaped
fruit; more hope knocked from the trees
of our tomorrow. Therefore, when surrounded
by the soft clarity of light, despite
steadying wonder's blade on my tongue
to pollard the heart, I still shiver at
the vastness of doubts blooming in my mouth.
We never set out to reseed our shame.
We failed to imagine this bounty
of home-shaped questions with no relief.
We keep wanting forgiveness to yield
the next belonging from our fallow breath.

Family-Portrait With Labor

I.

                    After the drugs—though maybe
before all else, because even my boundless image
of him holding a crack pipe was crafted
from the unrefined ugliness of his absence:

my father's hands mean *work*. Through the severe
safety of a silence I once planted between us,
my own hired soreness grew into a warm-blooded shrug
for his difficult return. Thumbs struck while roofing

slammed open a suffering we could curse together
across the bitterness. I learned plumbing and
carried him home in palm-ache from the hours
of wrenching a way for water to join

and leave the unknown families. The summer I rolled
paint onto mortgaged houses, my father's strength
gathered beneath my grip like an old shadow or
a crooked smile. By now, any burn in the knuckles,

any flinch-reach from too much time spent pulling
something broken but necessary apart
for repair's half-answer feels like the next measure
in his lifelong dirge.   I'm writing a new song.

II.

We've sat down, my mother and I, to do the sorry math—
It always comes back a painful miracle: 1990s, mostly

single, four children, minimum wage, *work* the warmest
lullaby played on repeat, and her presence worn

thin but no ghost. There were the nights of her
cold crying into each emptiness she could hear

roaming the rooms of our house. There was
hunger and the homeless shelter. And there was

a fatigue that framed the youth and
beauty of her face like a coffin…

                                    Ma,
I'm trying to say I don't know how
to bless a secure music that,
for love, you made from your almost
not being here. I still carry the key
and seal of it.   Yet I fear all
your body has lost and not
recovered. Time, for instance, and good rest.
I want a knell brighter than death between you
and retirement. I listen for the hymn or
horizon that draws more light than need
toward your tomorrow—more faith and some paid-off,
open place to prop the incredible tiredness of your feet
above your tired and incredible heart.

Self-Portrait With Stingers

Sometimes I question the blessing of each window
opened to pain's awkward but certain
        approach, of rewriting my name in tenderness

without converting this body to smoke.   The first hit:
        I watched what I didn't know then
to be a yellowjacket alight in my preschool palm

        as instinct curled fingers around the pleasant
tickle of six whispery legs within my grasp…
        Years later, I nearly lost an eye for trying my own

foolish hand at defending. After the dog had nosed the beehive
        tucked in rose bushes and came out a yelping
twisting thing, I took up arms—I didn't see

        the hit coming: not through the veil of youth;
not while hurling at the hive any branch I could raise;
        and not when, out of everything to launch but anger,

I belly crawled beneath the thick buzz of danger
        in the air. What made me stand the moment I'd gained
a misfired branch, lifting the enemy of my head

        with its too-few memories and brown irises
into a cloud of sharp answers?   Years later, by luck, I got
        stung by what I didn't know could've been hundreds

of poisonous refusals to me, a boy-sized monster,
        treading on home—I didn't see the hit coming:
not while laboring to clear the field with my father,

whom even then I loved as terribly as I dreaded
his growing and not-yet-named discontent; not when
        shoulder to sweaty shoulder with him in the uneasy

togetherness of that difficult work; not until I
        trampled the belonging below and minor lightning
struck inside my pantleg, jolting me into the funniest

        unfunny jig of my life. I can still feel it:
my father's right-there face at the odd cusp of a laugh,
        but for the awful noise ruining with suffering

what was otherwise a quiet and beautiful boy. Years later,
        as luck would have it, I got stung once more
by what could've been a different multitude

        of murderous responses to me, this monster-
sized man, prodding at home—I didn't see the hit coming:
        not while prepping the path to paint

a neglected country cottage; not while teetering on my ladder
        to reach with paintbrush the final desiccated feet
of siding, which just so happened to hide something else's

        fiercely guarded safety, a secret my body was
the first to learn when that lightning struck again
        my back, the can I dropped adding its glossy contents

to the hard ground under what good light remained.   That
        was the last sting I remember. Sometimes I forget
how steadily that venomous trouble would find me—season

        after season, until it suddenly stopped. Sometimes I fear
only this papery blockage keeping that old universe at bay,
        its litany of barbs carried my way on thin, elaborate wings.

To the Great Horned Owl

The fatherlessness I carry asks why
you would follow me, and then I learn how

you wing all across the Americas—
the way each miracle around us is

not the same understanding as witnessing
its barred but watching grace glide down

from another going day. You have always been
listening nearer than I realized.

I have always headed in your direction.
Even when I left the West, placing

the unspoken names of towns and woods
between me and the low-reaching true fir

where once you landed your tufted crown
only an impossible arm's length away,

the hard yellow glare of your eyes briefly
fixing my breath to awe's eternity

before you ascended through the old dark.
Back then, I accepted losing you

as my car climbed into the Alleghenies.
Until, against the shrill cicadas' constant

singing, lightning bugs constellating
fields like I'd never seen, the first night-sound

to grip me with the eeriness of belonging
was the deep timbre of your hoot out over

the Susquehanna waters, my life suddenly
mantled by a new horizon, ending unknown.

Hearth

—for my son

Tonight, a storm. And I hear weak humming
drift down the throat of this rain-voiced house.
My son is asleep when I check, but the first notes
sounded like the softness of him upstairs
learning by singing to soothe his own doubts.
I've answered that hymnal despair before;
I've been that odd wonder—no hidden talent,
just the boy who, if asked, would let a room
of unhomed siblings hear him trying to hush
the terror his own mind could not contain
but for song. Nightmares taught me young.
When the pale lady from my dreaming began
to blur with waking life, for days I trembled
through the winded dark of our tired trailer
to know the frightening figure had not
returned for my family. I whispered strange
psalms from bed to bed, window to window
banishing fear's face. I must have sung.
I can't imagine me back without the singing.
So, I tell any self not yet tucked inside a warm
if dreamless rest: *Sing for home. Sing, then sleep.*

Hush Now

—after Davis McCombs

As the last snowfall frames this year
in its radical quiet, I feel more

parent than ever and my closest to claiming
a survived living, yet I can't seem to call the sad-boy search

off; the porchlight tripped by my father's
addiction remains wired with a hope I have not

shed. Truth be told, the slightest breeze-shift
beyond the heart's barricade will set me

to picking locks I built in all the miracle shapes
of his leaving. I can still trace my high-pitched

whisper for him to wander back to the pale pickup
he locked me in, a crooked love's length

from his dealer, as the worst of desire finished
adding him to the dark. Who am I without a father-

sized hole inside my wondering? Who am I
even talking to—by now I have invented more

resurrections than he ever performed
before or after the gravity of his going. Happy

youth that I couldn't be. Happy then dream.
By wanting him something holier than absent,

I learned I could die of waiting for the warmth
in a name no prayer would revive. When the snow

completes the natural song of its weepy vanishing, I swear
the wind carries fragments of some plea far off and small

enough to sound like the abandoned boy in my voice
asking not-quite-himself if he will outlive this terror.

Father? was how he managed this uncertainty's path
through the rawness of his throat back then. And as

memory wafts, I understand what boy-me maybe heard
all those years ago—first as despair, so daunted by distances

as the boy was, and then as a kind of mercy—because here I am,
murmuring back to the edge in his worry: not *Father*, but

Farther, farther, casting tears now across the melt-music and
believing again in a love as deep as my biding for the boy to arrive.

Crow

—to the child survivor that lives in me

Dearness—My hand won't stop brushing the rough
bark of the redbud you didn't believe
we'd live to see flower again. And I can smell
the windfallen leaves involved in the dark work
we still have left before we embrace
in the one night all bodies must lie down in.

But not today. Today the neighborhood crows
and traveling geese are singing of arrival: *We made it!*
We made it!—thin light slanting gently through
this busy air. Thank you for filling up
our lungs between each suffering back then,
for giving us what we needed to get

here, where I pick one of this season's last
edible seeds just to feel your smile's old
rarity stumble across the quiet
warmth of my mouth's stage. Often, we were racked
with unthinkable grief, and more sorrow
is surely on its way. But we were blessed

by something, too. And today the soft light,
the coarse tree with its crisp pods, the singing
wind, and this absurd swell of gratitude
for how you outlived the awful wait
that fear can make of longing—which, I've come
to assure you, we find bright ways to survive.

What's Broken

—after Dorianne Laux

The river's long face. Middle eye
of a flyrod left behind by the dead.

The porch-window's screen,
giving mosquitos their straight shot

to the family blood. As a teenager,
at once, my right hand and my mother's

trove of knick-knack magnets
after I became another rogue wave

of rage against the empty fridge. Broken
the glass tabletop, the basement door,

and the toilet's grip on the tile floor.
Years ago, the first spell of parenthood

snapped when the sonogram failed
to flicker. And then cancer downed

the dream of yoking more laden branches
to the lineage tree. *What hasn't*

been rent, divided, split? Broken
the garden-fairy's porcelain wings

after falling from the fountain's edge.
The fickle coffee pot, from love,

when my rainbow boy added water
to the wrong channel, in hopes

of coaxing me from bed. Broken
the mythic singularity of meaning

and one day, perhaps, my fear of moving
through time as if pain could revive

any terror from the moony past.
Just this morning, I felt something

give a little while walking the child along
the sidewalk's unevenness, buckled

by the old roots below, our chatter's glint
cut short by the yellow arrival of his bus

and our rushed kissing goodbye.

Bringing Things Near

Something of the wind's way with trees right now,
   its moment to moment renaming of what
earlier I mistook as flowered stillness
   and not so much reaching for sky, branches
wavering into this then that airspace,

   hewing a fresh door from my wonder
just rough and faithful enough for mercy's
   warmth to maybe flutter through, until—yes,
there you come, that vast smile of yours, unchanged
   somehow by time or silence…

Of course, I'm only weaving another surrogacy
   out of the wind. Some mercies never arrive.
Why then, before the next breath fails to conjure,
   do I keep feeling one wild word away
from awe with wings as slick as any ruin?

Elegy With Its Breath Knocked Out

—for M.H. (1977-2022)

Is that the flute of your voice at my heart

daring to spill one more sobering truth?

Is that my anger's ghost shaking my head?

Is that loneliness confusing the point?

Of course, it isn't.   Of course, it is.

Requiem With Remission

—for L

After another last surgery. After
hearing her wake late within the breached levee

of her whole life. After water-hymn, as I
washed her body's sutured beauty, the blade

of doubt in both our faces whetted once again
by the word *cancer*. After our child had grasped

at the warmth in her palm and led her out
to watch the remaining spring light

moving cardinals between the Ozark oaks
early in their season of going golden-green.

After I was alone and the softness
from a radio song invited me

to ask for a little mercy now. And when
this question made of my throat a sieve

that could catch no grief—She kind of
found me like that, adding the mereness

of my tears to the half-cleaned dishes
inside the sink. Then our child's far-off voice

returned us to the more bearable shape
of our actual sadness. That night—

together in the yard and not much wind
combing through and no firefly wonder

for the child to waft at—a feared departure
still hovered ghost-close. But for the next

holy hour or so, we would not wander
beyond the gathering we'd dreamt, just yet.

Ever After

Only LOVE / has turned some turbulence with light into my tenderness for the shadows flailing inside most hearts.

Only LOVE / let this tendency to query the dark grow good reasons to bow before the curiosity that will visit my son's beautiful face, reinventing his whole life sometimes.

At night, only LOVE / could tether my tired mind to the brief history of our belonging.

Only LOVE / called it *family*.

Only LOVE / asked me to trust a desire with crescents of doubt lit between my teeth.

And only LOVE / delivered a better literacy: literacy of the dearly distanced; of the just-turned-out lamp; of the child's following breath, which I will not always survive (*Amen*); of any instinct that almost passes for clarity; of another bird's final arc for living half its nobility in falling; of whatever provokes the next prayer to cross the next drought in proof; of you, Dear Reader, and the halo of your attention lingering in the doorway like this. (Why have you done that now? For whom?)

And when I'm nearly out of names for the ever-chord of possibility (hope's hush?) sounding the dumbstruck of my being here, only LOVE / brightens something else between us I've never heard before. It hums like mercy.

But, Please, Not Too Soon...

—for K

One day: there will be another
rebounding forest flared by fireweed
& yellow wood sorrel, the light burden
of their edible blooms outliving us.

There will be wind sometimes
entangling the acoustic leaves
& sweeping away the largeness of a quiet
for which we were never responsible.

No need to recover. No need to tend
those grounds for survivors who may stumble
into a healing forest as if the wilderness
of their own grief, the edge of their breathing

softened some by the sighs inside
any singing we will have left behind.

When I Wasn't Vanishing

—for my sister

I tried paying attention to my life—the one
I could live and not whatever common
or uncommon wreckage kept insisting

was mine. But that grace only kindled
from wisps of what felt, at first,
like fiction: *My days will hold more magic*

than suffering, right? The truth is, for years
I believed in all the badness
I had lived. Then a blue voice that was

maybe just the wind started this quiet
story about passing through
one valley's darkness as morning

adorned that glade's depressions
with a little light. Slowly, my nights
seemed bordered by wonder, and I hummed

when necessary, until the sun again,
or something like it glistened
the image of my living for a while.

For the Cold That Gets In,
For the Cold We Keep Out

—for M

May we track a revival   through the next dark.
May we add its beating aperture inside our voices.
May we go silent before a sunrise while stalking some
winter body that seems static—like this freezing forest
of slender cedar & secret deer—just to see the light
pooling then plunging whatever we can know of
hungers roaming there all along: distinction,
a miracle in slow & sudden stages. Same
with each windy feeling that floods
or drains our chambers. Like joy.
Like change. Like peace.
All we might want
our living
to be.

Hymn at My Throat

—after Amanda Shires

Another bird tucks the gray flute of its body
through a tree's tangle of dusky branches, and
the boy at the desk of my heart starts.

The boy at my heart's desk removes the #2 pencil
he's been worrying between his teeth to open
the final sentence for his essay on love: *Dear bird
of light that lives in me…*

The boy pushes an awkward cursive toward the end
of something you could call prayer because
moments ago the darkness made him fear to finish
what he needed to ask me about loneliness.

But then a weeping I never felt lessen—it just
walked away—raises its voice again along the halls
of memory, and the boy aims his eraser
at everything before.

                    Another bird tucks the gray
of its body through a tree's tangled branches,
and the boy at the desk of my heart stops.

Inside the Charged Dark

Dear Mother,

Your early lessons got me to bear the fearful sounds
that faith can make while clearing its throat. I remember

the hard man who reaped our purpling timothy-grass
each spring unbuttoning his tanned jacket to show

a gray kitten, gunky-eyed and nestled against fleece lining.
I remember reaching with hesitation while saying

her new name. As she grew into cat, I have no memory
of feeling her claws. Maybe that was when I started

begging to keep buried in me what can hurt? I would never
see her outdoors again, but she must have answered

the barn cats singing to her readiness for life. You gave me
the word *pregnant* and a story for the act on its way.

I remember it was night. I remember trusting your insistence
to leave her alone to the body-work as we prepared

a toweled box in the nearby privacy of the closet.
You drifted toward sleep, and I forget how many times I rose

and returned her to that darkness before submitting
to her urge to burrow beneath the low canopy my knees

were making of my blankets. In bed with this restless wonder,
I heard a sound I knew but not, because it seemed to come

from some strange shore I couldn't find. Until I could:
the mewing blindness of her first kitten's head transforming

the old boundary of her body. I cried out, certain she was
becoming my failure to keep her locked inside the charged dark,

my betrayal breaking her into something, I still don't
have the words. Without language or understanding, I'd made

a hideous world. I was hideous and crying—
then the warm safety of your *hush* was suddenly there,

softening the cave of uncertainty at my ear,
leading me back into my chance to see I would survive

looking a blessing in its full face before believing
I deserved the voice of light.

Unfinished

Despite losing the dining table to it
for weeks, our family stays
with the puzzle, teetering plates
upon knees before the television
and then returning to the soft symphony
of shifting the oneness of a cardboard shape
into the satisfied oneness of another,
over and over, the thousand little clicks
of pleasure.   —More than that
if you count how, from time to time,
someone will recognize the need
to undo what we took for perfection
but what, in fact, was silently stalling
the possibility of seeing the thing
through, until someone else
or that same someone plucks out
the problem piece, resetting the bell
for an actual perfect.   *Family, isn't this*
what we're after? no one says, all hunched
and humming above the unfinished quiet
that buoys our separate, shared work.

Notes

"Time Can't Erase, Together": This poem takes its title from lyrics in Heatwave's song "Look After Love" on the album *Current* (Epic, 1982)—though, I first heard these lyrics sampled on an Aaron May track called "Let Go."

"Longing, We Say": This poem takes its title from a line in Robert Hass's poem "Meditation at Lagunitas" in the collection *Praise* (Ecco, 1979).

"Loom": The epigraph to this poem comes from Jack Gilbert's "Failing and Flying" in the collection *Refusing Heaven* (Knopf, 2005).

"It Must Have Been Summer": This poem holds tight to the structural (and thematic) hand of Dorianne Laux's poem of the same title in the collection *Facts About the Moon* (W. W. Norton & Company, 2005).

"Hush Now": This poem is in concert with Davis McCombs's poem "Sight Unseen" in the collection *Lore* (University of Utah Press, 2016).

"Hearth": This poem is in concert with Caitlyn Curran's poem "I Am Not Your Aunt" in the collection *With Midnight Down Your Throat* (Willow Springs Books, 2022).

"What's Broken": This poem holds tight to the structural (and thematic) hand of Dorianne Laux's poem of the same title in the collection *Facts About the Moon* (W. W. Norton & Company, 2005). The italicized language also comes from that Laux poem.

"Hymn at My Throat": This poem takes its title from a lyric on the title track of Amanda Shires' album *Take It Like a Man* (ATO Records, 2022).

Acknowledgments

My deep appreciation to the editors of these venues for showing belief in this work by publishing earlier versions of poems:

AGNI: "*Time Can't Erase, Together*";

The Atlantic: "Requiem With Remission" and "Unfinished";

Crashtest: "Hush Now";

The Massachusetts Review: "Bringing Things Near";

Orion Magazine: "Hearth";

Oxford American: "Separated";

Ploughshares: "From the Midnight Notebooks";

Poetry International: "Crow";

Southern Indiana Review: "But, Please, Not Too Soon…";

Swamp Pink: "Self-Portrait With Waiting" and "Mercy from the Orchard";

Traverse: "*Longing, We Say*" and "Self-Portrait With Stingers."

"Family-Portrait With Labor" first appeared under a different title in *What Things Cost: An Anthology for the People* (University Press of Kentucky), edited by Rebecca Gayle Howell and Ashley M. Jones, with Emily Jalloul.

"To the Great Horned Owl" first appeared in *A Literary Field Guide to Northern Appalachia* (University of Georgia Press), edited by Noah Davis, Todd Davis, and Dr. Carolyn Mahan.

"When I Wasn't Vanishing" first appeared as a broadside published by Broadsided Press.

It is a tremendous honor to hold a place within the luminous house of BOA Editions.

This work was made possible through vibrant support from a wide range of communities including the Cave Canem Foundation, the Historic Cane Hill Nature Writing Workshop, the National Endowment for the Arts, the Omega Institute for Holistic Studies, the *Orion* Environmental Writers' Workshop, The Rainier Writing Workshop, The University of Arkansas Program in Creative Writing & Translation, my Spring 2023 Undergraduate Writing Workshop, and The Writers' Colony at Dairy Hollow.

Nothing happens alone. Bless Robin Becker. Bless Julia Spicher Kasdorf. Bless Dorianne Laux. Bless Jane Blunschi. Bless Davis McCombs. Bless Rebecca Gayle Howell. Bless Liz Bradfield. Bless Rachel Mennies. Bless F. Douglas Brown. Bless Padma. Bless Geoff. Bless Toni. Bless Bryan and John. Bless Jackie. Bless Keetje and Erika. Bless Jefe and Lynne and Adam. Bless James. Bless Steve. Bless Meg and Laura and Katie and Emily and Annie and Zan and Riley and Robin and Remi and Elizabeth and Lynn and Aaron. Bless Katrina and Michael. Bless Katie and Moira. Bless Cynthia. Bless Lori.

Bless Ramona. Bless Nikki. Bless Cary and Edwin. Bless my beloved nieces and nephews, the lights that they are always becoming and the lights that brought them into this world. And somehow still, bless my father.

If there is an above all: Bless Carlos, bless him.

And there are folks I've left unnamed or surely forgotten: I'm sending an abiding love to them, too. I carry a bright constellation of gratitude for everyone who has offered some kind of faith in this necessary stumbling through poetry—I feel cared for and kept by that collective imagination.

Again, I don't know how or whether to apologize to those who have been called here to testify under the liberal subpoena of creativity, but I hope any reader will realize this book's affection, if fraught, for all its figures, as well as my unfinished understanding of the pain I can put folks to in the many numinous names of love.

About the Author

Geffrey Davis is the author of two previous books: *Night Angler* (BOA Editions, 2019), winner of the James Laughlin Award from the Academy of American Poets; and *Revising the Storm* (BOA, 2014), winner of the A. Poulin, Jr. Poetry Prize and a finalist for the Hurston/Wright Legacy Award. A recipient of the Anne Halley Poetry Prize, the Dogwood Prize in Poetry, the Porter Fund Literary Prize, and the Wabash Prize for Poetry, Davis has also received fellowships from Bread Loaf, Cave Canem, the National Endowment for the Arts, the Vermont Studio Center, and the Whiting Foundation for his involvement with The Prison Story Project, which strives to empower incarcerated women and men to tell their own stories through writing. His poems have been published by *The Atlantic, New England Review, The New York Times Magazine, The New Yorker, Orion Magazine, Oxford American,* PBS NewsHour, *Ploughshares,* and elsewhere. Davis currently lives in the Ozarks, where he teaches full-time with the University of Arkansas's Program in Creative Writing & Translation. Raised by the Pacific Northwest, he also serves as Poetry Editor for *Iron Horse Literary Review* and is a core faculty member of The Rainier Writing Workshop.

BOA Editions, Ltd. American Poets Continuum Series

Colophon

BOA Editions, Ltd., a not-for-profit publisher of poetry
and other literary works, fosters readership and appreciation
of contemporary literature. By identifying, cultivating, and publishing both new and
established poets and selecting authors of unique literary talent, BOA brings high-
quality literature to the public.
Support for this effort comes from the sale of its publications, grant funding, and
private donations.

The publication of this book is made possible, in part,
by the special support of the following individuals:

Anonymous

Angela Bonazinga & Catherine Lewis

Bernadette Catalana

Daniel R. Cawley

Margaret B. Heminway

Charles Hertrick & Joan Gerrity

Nora A. Jones

Keetje and Sarah Kuipers

Paul LaFerriere & Dorrie Parini, *in honor of Bill Waddell*

Jack & Gail Langerak

Barbara Lovenheim

Joe McElveney

Daniel M. Meyers, *in honor of J. Shepard Skiff*

John H. Schultz

William Waddell & Linda Rubel

Michael Waters & Mihaela Moscaliuc